KILLER WHALES

— BUILT FOR THE HUNT —

by Christine Zuchora-Walske

Consultant: Dr. Jackie Gai, DVM

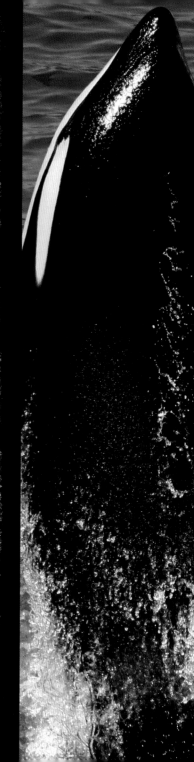

Raintree is an imprint of Capstone Global Library Limited, a company incorporated in England and Wales having its registered office at 264 Banbury Road, Oxford, OX2 7DY – Registered company number: 6695582

www.raintree.co.uk
myorders@raintree.co.uk

Editorial Credits
Brenda Haugen, editor; Kazuko Collins and Juliette Peters, designers; Tracy Cummins, media researcher; Katy LaVigne, production specialist

Printed and bound in China.

ISBN 978 1 474 70199 0 (hardback)
19 18 17 16 15
10 9 8 7 6 5 4 3 2 1

ISBN 978 1 474 70206 5 (paperback)
20 19 18 17 16
10 9 8 7 6 5 4 3 2 1

British Library Cataloguing in Publication Data
A full catalogue record for this book is available from the British Library.

Photo Credits
Getty Images: Fleetham Dave, 21, Gerard Soury, 15, Greg Johnston, 19; iStockphoto: sethakan, 8; Minden Pictures: Sue Flood, 17; Shutterstock: Doptis, 1, Ferderic B, 2, Back Cover, Monika Wieland, 7, 16, pashabo, Design Element, Tatiana Ivkovich, 3, TOSP, Cover; Thinkstock: Christian Musat, 11, Evgeniya Lazareva, 6, jonmccormackphoto, 5, NicolA!s MeroAo, 13, S_Lew, 12, Tatiana Ivkovich, 9.

CONTENTS

MIGHTY HUNTERS

Killer whales are deadly **predators**. They live in all of the world's oceans. Killer whales hunt seals, penguins, fish and other animals. They use teamwork and a sharp sense of hearing to find **prey**. Their size and strength help them to attack and kill their prey. Killer whales can eat as much as 227 kilograms (500 pounds) of food in one day!

FACT

Killer whales are also called orcas.

predator animal that hunts other animals for food

prey animal hunted by another animal for food

ALL IN THE FAMILY

Killer whales live in family groups called **pods**. A pod may have more than 30 whales. Pod members usually work together to find and kill prey. Young killer whales learn to hunt by copying the actions of their older **relatives**.

FACT
A killer whale pod always has a female leader.

pod group of whales

relative family member

SPEEDY AND STRONG

Killer whales are built for chasing and killing. They have strong, smooth bodies that move through the water quickly. They can swim up to 45 kilometres (28 miles) per hour. They are also huge. They are bigger and heavier than most cars! Their large size helps them to overpower smaller animals.

SEARCHING BY SOUND

Killer whales **communicate** when they hunt together. They whistle and make calls, pops and jaw claps. These sounds help them to hunt as a team. Killer whales also use **echolocation**. They click and listen for echoes. From the echoes, killer whales can determine the size, shape and location of prey.

FACT

Killer whales have no sense of smell.

communicate share thoughts, feelings or information

echolocation use of sounds and echoes to locate objects such as food

HIDING IN OPEN SEA

A killer whale's colouring hides it from prey. It can sneak up on prey from above or below. From above, a killer whale's black back looks like the dark water below. From below, the killer whale's white belly looks like the sunshine above.

FACT

A killer whale's colouring confuses prey. It cannot see the whale's shape clearly.

MANY WAYS TO CATCH A MEAL

Killer whales are hunters. They may chase sea **mammals** and trap them in a **bay**. If prey are sitting on sea ice, killer whales bump the ice or make big waves. The killer whales knock the prey into the water, where they can attack. Killer whales also slide onto sea ice and beaches to hunt penguins and seals.

mammal warm-blooded animal that breathes air; mammals have hair or fur; female mammals feed milk to their young

bay part of the ocean that is partly closed in by land

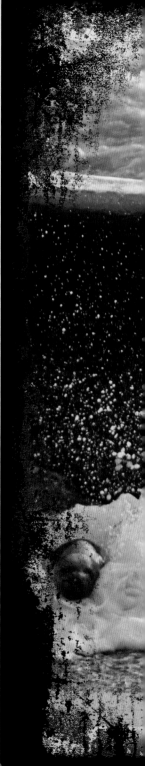

Killer whales kill prey in different ways. They often circle small prey such as fish. The whales attack when the fish are trapped. To kill a big whale, killer whales attack it from all sides. Killer whales force sharks to the surface, where the sharks cannot breathe. They hit the sharks with their tails to stun them before eating them.

A pod of killer whales attacks a grey whale.

JAWS of DEATH

A killer whale's mouth is deadly. Its jaws are big and strong. It has up to 52 pointy teeth. Each tooth is as long as an adult human finger! The teeth lock together and help the killer whale to grip and tear its prey.

FACT

Killer whales are born with all the teeth they will ever have.

LONG LIVE THE KILLER WHALE

Killer whales are deadly hunters that can live a long time. Some killer whales live for up to 90 years! Because they are so large, few other animals dare to attack them.

AMAZING BUT TRUE!

A killer whale can never fall completely asleep because it has to think about breathing. Only half of its brain can rest at a time. The other half of the brain stays awake. It helps the killer whale to remember to breathe, and to watch and listen for danger.

GLOSSARY

bay part of the ocean that is partly closed in by land

communicate share thoughts, feelings or information

echolocation use of sounds and echoes to locate objects such as food

mammal warm-blooded animal that breathes air; mammals have hair or fur; female mammals feed milk to their young

pod group of whales

predator animal that hunts other animals for food

prey animal hunted by another animal for food

relative family member

READ MORE

Animals that Hunt (Adapted to Survive), Angela Royston (Raintree, 2014)

Ocean Food Chains (Food Chains and Webs), Angela Royston (Raintree, 2014)

Orcas (Animal Abilities), Anna Claybourne (Raintree, 2014)

WEBSITES

www.bbc.co.uk/nature/life/Killer_whale

Learn more about killer whales.

www.bbc.co.uk/nature/life/Cetacea

Learn more about whales, dolphins and porpoises.

COMPREHENSION QUESTIONS

1. How many teeth does a killer whale have? How do they use their teeth when hunting prey?

2. What senses do killer whales use to hunt for prey? Which sense do you think it would be the hardest to go without? Why?

INDEX